Horoscopes & Astrology 2022

Snake

By: Zhouyi Feng Shui

OCEAN SPIRIT
HEART IS YOUR COMPASS
N
W
E
S
19
91
IN THE JOURNEY OF LIFE
BORN TO BE FREE

Table of Contents

Introduce

People born in the year of the Snake are wise. Intelligent, capable, ambitious, adaptable to all situations with high ability. Love someone who really loves not flirting, but rather loves strength, hates force, knows how to plan and is patient, has psychology, is charming. Have human relations, can easily get along with others, good-hearted, compassionate. Outwardly, you look stern and tidy, but you're a deep, calm person who loves to learn about everything.

Because persons born in the year of the Snake are fire-elemental, you should work in the fire industry. For instance, you may create a store that sells electrical or electronic equipment such as radios and televisions, or you could offer other electrical appliances. Open a gas station, build a gas station, or pursue a career that requires specific skills, such as being a speaker, critic, judge, prosecutor, teacher, writer, politician, journalist, beautician, photographer, makeup artist, model, selling artificial plants, artificial flowers, or fortune-tellers in various fields, soldiers, or police.

Year of the Snake (Gold Element) (1941) & (2001)

"Hibernating Snake" Those born in the Year of the Snake, 81 years old (1941) and the age cycle of 21 years (2001)

Overall Horoscope

Because the planet rotating into your destiny this year is the "star across the sky," this year is another year in which you should take extra care of your health because it may cause issues for the senior destiny around the age of 81. Food hygiene is very important, as is avoiding hot foods and visiting a doctor for regular check-ups. Furthermore, you should avoid interfering with other people's issues. You should be blessed if you are very picky with children and grandkids who visit you. Your family and close friends will respect and adore you as well.

It is another year that the event will find a

patron for destiny around the age of 21, thanks to getting auspicious power from the Virtue Star. The research will proceed for those of you who run your own business to get the desired results. To increase knowledge, however, every labor activity must be rigorous and persistent. Adapt your technique plan to the circumstances. Avoid becoming entangled in non-business matters and keep an eye out for accidents while on the road. Be wary of slanderous individuals. If a buddy asks you to an orbit, you should decline, and you must be able to manage your emotions.

Because Lord Tai Tribute's strength will collide with the two destinies of this year's age. You should set aside time at the start of the year to pay tribute to the Tai Swe Yee deity and pray for his favor to protect you from tragedy.

Career

For the future of the young, There will be growth this year, whether you are working or operating a business, or whether you are in higher education. You have the option to study both at home and abroad this year. and will have a bright future in a decent job If you start working this year, the elders will help you, especially in the month that supports you, including the 2nd month of China (5 Mar. – 4 Apr.), the 4th month of China (5 May – 5 June) 6th month of China (7 Jul. – 6 Aug.) and 7th month of China (7 Aug. – 6 Sep.)

Any job or investment for young people this year should be properly researched, especially contract contracts. To obtain experience, you should be humble rather than arrogant and arrogant, since this would prohibit you from gaining good possibilities. Especially during the 3rd month of China (5 Apr. – 4 May), 8th month of China (7 Sep. – 7 Oct.), 9th month of China (8 Oct. – 6 Nov.), and the 11th month of China (7 Dec. – 4 Jan. 23) in any job. You must adhere to society's and the law's norms. You must use extreme caution in your work since you have the right to be fooled or exploited.

Wealth

The financial fortunes of this year have taken a turn for the worst. Expenditures are high, while income is decreasing. You have the right to a negative practically every month, it may be stated. If you can't make more money, the greatest thing you can do is cut back on your spending. to maintain a healthy financial situation You should not pay for anything that is not required and instead save. And you'll need to keep saving to cover any unforeseen bills that may arise, squeezing your cash flow even more. Especially during the 3rd month of China (5 Apr. − 4 May), the 8th month of China (7 Sep. − 7 Oct.), the 9th month of China (8 Oct. − 6 Nov.), and the 11th month of China (7 Dec. − 4 Jan. 23).

As for the month in which the financial flow is smooth, it is the 2nd month of China (5 Mar. − 4 Apr), the 4th month of China (5 May − 5 June), the 6th month of China (7 Jul −). 6 Aug.) and 7th month of China (7 Aug. − 6 Sep.).

Family
The good and the terrible will be blended in this year's family horoscope. However, if an auspicious occurrence occurs in your home, it will assist to alleviate the negative aspects,

but there are certain things to be aware of. Concerns for the safety of family members and the elderly's disease You should also be mindful that a youngster or a servant can hurt you. Be especially cautious about lost valuables during China's 3rd month (5 April – 4 May), 8th month (7 September – 7 October), 9th month (8 October – 6 November), and 11th month (7 December – 4 January). Theft or home invasion, caring for sick individuals in the house, and work-related accidents are all risks to be aware of. However, in terms of family and friends, this year seems promising. Many close pals will assist you. To achieve the aim, make what is anticipated and intended.

Lover

In terms of this year's Elder Fate, you must avoid interfering or being overly concerned about your kids. It will also be revered and adored by youngsters.

This is a year of enormous allure for young people. The opposite sex will pay you a lot of attention. But don't get too impatient. It is not too late to be in a heartfelt relationship and have a positive attitude before waiting to be certain. Then gradually advance the relationship to the next level. You must also understand restraint.

Importantly, you need to know restraint, especially during the 3rd month of China (5 Apr - 4 May.), the 8th month of China (7 Sep. - 7 Oct.), the 9th month of China (8 Oct. – 6 Nov.) and the 11th month of China (7 Dec. – 4 Jan. 23), when you must be careful not to let the atmosphere cause damage. Don't be too conceited, since if something bad occurs to you, you'll lose your job, and don't become involved in your friend's love relationships.

Health

This year's seniors' health is not in excellent shape. will quickly become unwell As a result, you should get enough rest. Food that is easy to digest and helpful should be prioritized. It will not be necessary to forfeit possessions to preserve illness immunity. Especially during the 3rd month of China (5 Apr. – 4 May), the 8th month of China (7 Sep. – 7 Oct.), the 9th month of China (8 Oct. – 6 Nov.), and the 11th month of China (7 Dec. – 4 Jan.23). Aches and pains, bone pains, or fainting should all be avoided since they will lead you to fall and damage you. Also, if you have diabetes or heart problems, you should exercise caution.

Lucky Numbers

8	1	8
2	2	2
4	0	8

Annual sacred objects for the Snake: "Guan Yu God bestows wealth"

Residents: Auspicious objects should be placed in the North.
Shops or workplaces: should set sacred objects in the South.

* Should set the sacred object in the direction specified or facing the deity towards the door

Year of the Snake (Water Element) (1953)

"Snake in the grass" Those born in the Year of the Snake, 69 years old (1953) and age cycle 9 years (2013)

Overall Horoscope

The Virtue Star is the planet rotating into your destiny house this year for senior destiny. Chong Tai Tribute is due this year. As a result, you become irritated and grumpy. The greatest thing you can do this year is relaxing, avoid interfering with other people's issues, and avoid blaming your children or grandkids. Let's let certain things go. It will assist in making your mind feel more at ease. Another thing to keep in mind is that there are health conditions that will cost you a lot of money to address. Whether it's aches and pains in different joints or frequent cramping, stay on the lookout for hidden disorders. As a result, you should consume nutritious foods. You should exercise modestly and visit your doctor regularly for check-ups. In addition, at the start of the year, opportunities to pay reverence to the gods and respect the Tai Swe Yee gods should be found. It will assist you in protecting your happiness from sickness, persecution, and many disasters.

For the future of the young, This year's star is the star across the sky, since circling stars transmit influence. This year, be wary of pals who try to convince you by playing video games all day. which, if consumed in excess, is detrimental to both study and health. Furthermore, be aware that while participating in outdoor activities, you may fall, become wounded, or lose possessions. Parents should take their children to pay homage to the Tai Swe Yee deity at the start of the year and pray for disaster protection.

Career

Seniors have a promising year ahead of them. There will be few difficulties and the capacity to deal with them when you are in charge. There are also individuals available to assist, but China must use caution while signing contract paperwork during the 3rd month (5

Apr. - 4 May). Do not rely on recommendations from family or friends. However, you should carefully review the subcontracting conditions to avoid future issues. Any work or investment you make this year should be thoroughly researched before proceeding. You have the right to damage yourself if you don't listen to persuasion and believe in simple persuasion. However, you should avoid during the 3rd month of china (5 Apr. – 4 May), the 8th month of china (7 Sep. – 7 Oct.), the 9th month of china (8 Oct. – 6 May). Oct.) and the 11th month of China (7 Dec. – 4 Jan.23). Be wary of greed traps that might take you down the wrong path or lead to accounting fraud.

For the sake of childhood's fate This year, it's important to be more vigilant to boost student interest in the lecture. Don't become addicted to the game or play it excessively. You will make significant progress this year if you have genuine ambitions. In terms of work and study, the is 2nd month of China (5 Mar – 4 Apr), 4th month of China (5 May – 5 Jun). 6th month of China (7 Jul. – 6 Aug.) and 7th month China (7 Aug. – 6 Sep.).

Wealth

Bad financial luck at the end of the year may be tough to get, but it will be more flexible towards the end of the year. Direct cash flow inflows as well as windfall cash flow inflows. You do not assign it for saving and investing if you have already received it. There's a risk there won't be anymore. Avoid current expenditures that may deplete your cash and create asset loss, especially during the 3rd month of China (5 Apr. - 4 May), the 8th month of China (7 Sept. - 7. Oct.), 9th month of China (8 Oct. – 6 Nov.), and 11th month of China (7 Dec. – 4 Jan. 23).

For the months that your finances will be smooth and flexible, namely, 2nd month of China (5 Mar. – 4 Apr.), 4th month of China (5 May. – 5th June), 6th month of China (7 Sep.) c. – 6 Aug.) and the 7th month of China (7 Aug. – 6 Sept.)

Family

His family's fortunes were not so favorable this year. There will be disagreements among the residents. On the side of the Elder Fate, be careful not to say anything that will make the children lose respect for you. As a result, it's advisable to play the role of counselor, offering advice and blessings when he arrives. You shouldn't make a big deal out of your personal feelings. It's also a good idea to stay out of your children's and grandchildren's personal affairs. Especially during the 3rd month, China (5 Apr. – 4 May), the 8th month of China (7 Sep. – 7 Oct.), the 9th month of China (8 Oct. – 6 Nov.), and the 11th month of China (7 Dec. – 4 Jan. 23).

This year will be enough for family and friends. You will be supported, and you will have the opportunity to reconnect with old friends and travel with them. There will be a chance to earn merit with family members or grandkids as well. This will assist in dissipating any negative energies and reducing the unevenness.

Lover
The love horoscope for this year isn't particularly promising, but there will be some clashing sounds, such as tongue and teeth. If you are prepared to compromise on certain issues, the opposing party will soon diminish

the violence. Try to be patient while you're unhappy. It is especially important to avoid violent quarrels during the 3rd month of China (5 Apr. – 4 May), 8th month of China (7 Sep. – 7 Oct.), 9th month of China (8 Oct. – 6 Nov.), and in the 11th month of China (7 Dec. – 4 Jan. 23). The best method is to stay out of other people's business. Be wary of the issues that occur as a result of your remarks.

Health

This year has not been kind to destiny's health. Seniors, in particular, will be sick, so ask for both old and new medicines. Back discomfort, lumbar pain, neck pain, and knee pain are two of the most common symptoms. However, there is something to be concerned about. Keep an eye out for ailments that aren't readily apparent. As a result, you should keep an eye on your body for any irregularities. If something goes wrong, you should see a doctor right away for a thorough evaluation.

The 3rd month of China (5 April – 4 May), the 8th month of China (7 Sept. – 7 Oct.), the 9th month of China (8 Oct. – 6 Nov.), and the 11th month of China (7 Dec. – 4 Jan.23) are not supportive and you should be particularly cautious about your health. You should schedule a check-up regularly. To stay fresh and clean, it's also critical that you take care of your head. Don't worry about things you can't control or that haven't arrived yet; instead, get adequate rest. and stringent about eating meals that are good for the body, as well as not meddling in other people's business Allowing yourself to let go will provide you peace of mind.

Playing with children should be done with

caution and safety in mind. Because falling can occasionally result in more serious injuries than you expect. As a result, you must use extreme caution.

Lucky Numbers

0	0	8
8	1	5
8	8	6

Annual sacred objects for the Snake: " Guan Yu God bestows wealth"

Residents: Auspicious objects should be placed in the southwest.

Shop or workplace: Auspicious objects should be placed in the northwest.

* Should set the sacred object in the direction specified or facing the deity towards the door

Year of the Snake (Fire Element) (1965)

"snake out of the cave " Those born in the Year of the Snake, 57 years old (1965)

Overall Horoscope

Because the planet that orbits into your destiny this year is a star in the sky, and persons born in the year of the Snake have a strong affinity with snakes. Lord Tai Tribute will bestow strength on yet another year of birth. As a result, this year will be a mixed bag of good and terrible for half of you. Sponsors will support and assist you in your line of employment or company. There will be a path to follow. However, it is up to you whether you make use of the excellent chance you have to create your work and make it helpful or not. You must be wary of the tiny ones or servants who defame and squander your fortune. However, looking on the positive side, this is a chance for you to strengthen yourself.

As a consequence, even if you are exhausted at work and home, the outcome of your exhaustion will be changed into work for you to enjoy later. So kindly wait for another year to pass. Your efforts will be rewarded.

Even if the lunar year was afflicted with power, he was lucky in comparison to other age groups. Because there are lucky stars to assist you to get through the hard times. However, health issues, disagreements, and audit difficulties should not be overlooked. Problems with government agencies should be avoided. You should go to the temple to pay your respects to the gods at the start of the year; paying your respects to the gods will aid in the smooth running of your business or trade.

Career

This year, as a result of the fortunate stars, there will be positive developments in your line of work or in the firm that you manage. There are ways to enhance earnings via producing outcomes, expanding commerce, and generating sales. So, if there is a good month, take advantage of it. You should move promptly to avoid missing out on this chance, especially during the months when your investing career is bright and lucrative, including the 2nd month of China (5 Mar. - 4 Apr.), the 4th month of China (5 May - 5 Jun.) 6th month of China (7 Jul. – 6 Aug.), and 7th month of China (7 Aug. – 6 Sep.)

However, if entering the 3rd month of China (5 Apr. – 4 May), 8th month, China (7 Sept. – 7 Oct.), 9th month of China (8 Oct. – 6 Nov.), and the 11th month of China (7 Dec. – 4 Jan.

23). You should be wary of youngsters or dependents who may cause problems. Also, be wary of contracts, since they may include hidden clauses. It has the purpose to fool you to deceive you and do harm, and be wary of internal disagreements and debates.

Support for participation in this year's joint venture will be found. The investment will pay off in the long run. But should be avoided during the 3rd month of China (5 Apr. – 4 May), 8th month of China (7 Sep. – 7 Oct.), 9th month of China (8 Oct. – 6 Nov.) and the 11th month of China (7 Dec. – 4 Jan. 23) should be avoided in case of accounting fraud or asset theft. As a result, please use extreme caution.

Wealth

This year's financial fortunes vary dramatically up and down, and he loses his seat. Working capital liquidity will be a challenge for several months of the year. You are affected by the crisis at various times. As a result, you should avoid taking up long-term debt this year. For example, auto payments, mortgage payments, and so on, because there will be more issues than previously. Especially during the 3rd month of China (5 Apr. – 4 May), the 8th month of China (7 Sep. – 7 Oct.), the 9th month of China (8 Oct. – 6 Nov.), and the 11th month of China (7 Dec. – 4 Jan. 23).

Loans and guarantees are not permitted at this time. Don't take chances with your luck. Do not invest in illicit enterprises or violate others' rights. Unnecessary costs should be reduced. You should plan how to utilize your money wisely at the start of the year and set aside a reserve for unexpected expenses.

Knowing how to restrict oneself and focus on sufficiency is preferable.

For the months that your finances will have better liquidity, namely, 2nd month of China (5 Mar. – 4 Apr.), 4th month of China (5 May. 5 Jun), 6th month of China (7 Jul. – 6 Aug.), and the 7th month of China (7 Aug. – 6 Sep.)

Family

If there is an auspicious occasion in your home this year. It will aid in the breakdown and relief of calamities. Something might not happen as planned if there is no auspicious occasion. Keep an eye on the children and the employees. raising a ruckus and inflicting property damage The destiny must be especially cautious about safety and accidents in the house during the 3rd month of China (5 Apr. – 4 May), 8th month of China (7 Sept. – 7 Oct.), 9th month of China (8 Oct. – 6

Nov.), and the 11th month of China (7 Dec. – 4 Jan.23). Keep an eye out for valuables that have been misplaced or stolen.

This year, be wary of family, friends, sweet-mouthed people, and sour-bottomed people. If you have to invest in stocks with family or friends, Make sure to thoroughly research the origins and prospects. Fear should not be used to enter the stock market or to invest. Both friendship and money will be lost in the end. You should also avoid getting engaged in disagreements with your friends. Especially during the bad months, namely, 3rd month of china (5 Apr. - 4 May), 8th month of china (7 Sept. - 7 Oct.), 9th month of china (8 Oct. - 6 Nov), and 11th month of china (7 Dec. – 4 Jan.).

Lover
Even though your love horoscope is poor this

year, there will always be a reason for you and your spouse to be skeptical of one another. As a result, you must ignore him and avoid making the gathering so formal that there is no time for family or loved ones. Finding time to share your dinner table or spend time together is a fantastic idea. Defend yourself by being honest. To break down the misunderstanding wall, you must also be tough and analytical rather than emotional. The months that you need to be very careful are: 3rd month of china (5 Apr. – 4 May), 8th month of china (7 Sept. – 7 Oct.), 9th month of china (8 Oct. . – 6 Nov), and 11th month of china (7 Dec. – 4 Jan. 23)

You must not meddle with other people's family matters during this time. Take caution not to start a fight. You should know how to protect yourself while going out to socialize or to entertainment places since you may become infected with the disease as a bonus.

Health

Your health is deteriorating. You should be mindful of digestive system disorders such as gastritis, intestinal illness, liver disease, and heart disease. As a result, you should take care of yourself by getting adequate rest and undertaking modest exercise regularly that is acceptable for your age. The month that you need to take extra care of your health is the 3rd month of China (5 Apr. - 4 May), 8th month of China (7 Sep. - 7 Oct.), 9th month of China (8 Oct. – 6 Nov.), and the 11th month of China (7 Dec. – 4 Jan. 23) where your health isn't doing so well. Fatigue should be avoided at all costs. Be on the lookout for fainting and accidents, as well as repeating prior ailments. You should also refrain from consuming alcoholic beverages.

Lucky Numbers

3	6	8
5	7	3
8	4	8

Annual sacred objects for the Snake: " Guan Yu God bestows wealth"

Residents: Auspicious objects should be placed in the west.

Shop or workplace: Auspicious objects should be placed in the east.

* Should set the sacred object in the direction specified or facing the deity towards the door

Year of the Snake (Earth Element) (1977)

" Snake in the Canal" Those born in the Year of the Snake, 45 years of age (1977)

Overall Horoscope

The Virtue Star is the planet that enters your

zodiac sign this year. As a consequence, many issues will be resolved smoothly this year. Even if your birthday is in a different year, you can still benefit from the Tai Shui gods' power. However, fortunate stars emerge in the zodiac signs and shine to help. As a result, if you are steady in virtue, hardworking, know how to add information, and react to the environment, your profession or trading business will progress, even if you are surrounded by numerous worries. However, you will finally be able to pass. Health, on the other hand, is a major issue for you this year. Liver illness, gastritis, intestinal disease, and food poisoning are all things to be wary of. They must also be extra cautious about accidents at work and on the road. Another thing to keep in mind is that this year's investments will be high-risk. As a result, you should exercise caution while investing. Also, avoid interfering in other people's business because there may be unintended consequences such as sorrow that you did not create, and be wary of lost goods.

The ideal approach to start the year is to

devote time to paying honor to sacred objects and paying respect to the deity Tai. To assist in the protection, dispersal, smoothing of commerce, and alleviation of catastrophes ranging from severe to minor.

Career

Because so many virtue stars and auspicious stars are moving across the zodiac line this year, it aids in the growth of your business. If you've planned something but haven't gotten around to it yet, consider your preparedness if numerous reasons come into play. This year will be an ideal moment for you to resurrect old initiatives and make progress. Because work and commerce will continue to advance positively. Especially during China's 2nd month (5 Mar. – 4 Apr.), 4th month (5 May – 5 Jun.), 6th month (7 Jul. – 6 Aug.), and 7th month (7 Aug. – 6 Sep.), but if it enters the 3rd month of China (5 Apr. – 4 May), the 8th month of China (7 Sep. – 7 Oct.), 9th month of China (8 Oct. – 6 Nov.), and 11th month of China (7 Dec. – 4 Jan. 23). Before you sign your endorsement, think about it carefully. You should also be aware of any internal issues in the company.

Wealth

This year, the financial horoscope is working against the job horoscope since there will be overflowing costs to keep up with the revenue, and it will frequently be the cause you did not expect. As a result, whatever money you may save should be used wisely. Don't waste too much time on frivolous stuff. Allow no one to borrow money or provide guarantees for family members. Both should refrain from gambling. Do not engage in illegal activities or infringe on others' rights. Because you may be punished and, more than likely, prosecuted. Especially the month that does not support you is the 3rd month of China (5 Apr. – 4 May), the 8th month of China (7 Sept. – 7 Oct.), the 9th month of China(8 Oct. – 6 Nov), and 11th month of China (7 Dec. – 4 Jan. 23)

As for the month in which your financial fortune is flowing well, it is the 2nd month of China (5 Mar. - 4 Apr.), 4th month of China (5 May. 5 Jun), 6th month of China (7 Jul. – 6

Aug.), and the 7th month of China (7 Aug. – 6 Sep.).

Family

Your family's fortunes are not looking good this year. Unexpected difficulties with the health and safety of individuals in the house may happen throughout the year, particularly incidents that might end in injury. In the house, both property loss and medical expenditures are incurred. Also, be aware of quarrels among family members, since they may quickly spread. Especially during the 3rd month of China (5 April – 4 May), the 8th month of China (7 Sep. – 7 Oct.), the 9th month of China (8 Oct. – 6 Nov.), and the 11th month of China (7 Dec. 65 – 4 Jan. 66), when you must be cautious of accidents in the house, especially with electrical appliances, gas stoves, or other flames. Thieves may break into your home, thus valuables must be safely safeguarded.

This is a bad year for family and friends. You must be wary of being assaulted or reprimanded by close friends or family members. In addition, if you're in the middle of a huge throng, If you're irritated or challenged in some way. If your impulsive reaction or emotional activity would lead you to suffer later, you must remain patient. Especially during the 3rd month of China (5 Apr. – 4 May), 8th month of China (7 Sep. – 7 Oct.), 9th month of China (8 Oct. – 6 Nov.), and the 11th month of China (7 Dec. – 4 Jan. 23), when it is completely forbidden for the destiny to be engaged in a friend's disagreement.

Lover

This year, your romantic side shines brightly. If you're single, people of the opposite sex who have a boyfriend or partner will get closer to you, and the lovers will pamper and care for each other as well. This year is ideal for taking a spouse on a sightseeing excursion to help refresh the mind or for bringing them to the temple to create merit, as this will assist to increase the love luck even more. However, fate should stay stable this year. When you walk outside, the opposite sex will become friends with you. Be wary of the other party's enchantment, which might result in people dying. Please keep in mind that fleeting bliss can lead to eternal family strife and disaster. As a result, I implore you to keep your sanity at all times. Especially during the 3rd month of China (5 Apr. – 4 May), the 8th month of China (7 Sept. – 7 Oct.), the 9th month of China (8 Oct. – 6 Nov.), and the 11th month of China (7 Dec. – 4 Jan. 23).

Health

Your health is suffering as a result of the Tai Shui gods' influence on your health issues. Especially stomach and intestinal problems, liver illness, and food poisoning. and be on the lookout for black headaches in the unsupported months, such as the 3rd month of China (5 Apr. - 4 May), the 8th month of China (7 Sep. - 7 Oct.), the 9th month of China (8 Oct. – 6 Nov.), and the 11th month of China (7 Dec. – 4 Jan. 23), when you should be extra cautious of accidents. When moving outside the home, stay wary of unexpected gunfire and avoid exhaustion till you pass out.

Lucky Numbers

2	8	9
3	5	8
4	7	5

Annual sacred objects for the Snake: " Guan Yu God bestows wealth"

Residents: Auspicious objects should be placed in the West.

Shop or workplace: Auspicious objects should be placed in the east.

** Should set the sacred object in the direction specified or facing the deity towards the door

Year of the Snake (Wood Element) (1989)

"Snake in the River" Those born in the Year of the Snake, 33 years old (1989)

Overall Horoscope

This year, the planet orbiting your life path is a star across the sky, providing a route of success and growth for destiny's company. The work will be scrutinized by the elders, allowing you to demonstrate your abilities and learn how to improve your work, assess your strengths and limitations, and identify career prospects. As a result, 2018 is a year of great opportunity. Destiny should be persistent and dedicated in creating works so that a bright future may be created that will benefit their well-being. But be careful because your work may be the envy of others. Therefore, if you do not know how to humble yourself, control your emotions, and your words, you will be subject to slander because the Year of the Snake is another zodiac sign that receives power from the Tai Shui gods. Therefore, for those of you who work in large roles, please be careful in doing different things. Everything has to be transparent with reasons to explain. Otherwise, the ill-wishers will have the opportunity to cut the legs of your chair. This year, to roam in entertainment or socialize in orbit. There may be a punishment that makes you suffer. At the beginning of the year you should find time to pay respects to the Tai Tribe gods to help keep things smooth, business progress, and trade prosperous. May destiny be diligent in making merit and making merit. It will help alleviate the disaster from heavy to light.

Career

Even though trade will progress this year, there will be a chance to expand. However, you should think about this carefully before acting, as there are additional risk variables outside your control. Success, on the other hand, is not far away. If you're not sloppy, you'll be OK. But entering the 3rd month of China (5 Apr. – 4 May), 8th month of China

(7 Sept. – 7 Oct.), 9th month of China (8 Oct. – 6 Nov.), and the 11th month of China (7 Dec. – 4 Jan.23), Where deception has the potential to harm investments or joint ventures. You should also be mindful of market or product instability, as well as the fall of domestic and international economic systems, which can result in losses.

The months in which your work and investment will be bright are the 2nd month of China (5 Mar.-4 Apr), 4th month of China (5 May - 5 Jun), 6th month of China (7 Jul. – 6 Aug.), and the 7th month of China (7 Aug. – 6 Sep.).

Wealth

Your financial fortune is empty this year, which means that your income and spending are the same, there is no money left over, and you are not saving. Finances can be a problem. As a result, please be frugal. Unnecessary costs are being requested to be cut. It's essential to stick to the sufficiency concept and start accumulating money initially. such as the 3rd month of China (5 Apr. – 4 May), the 8th month of China (7 Sept. – 7 Oct.), the 9th month of China (8 Oct.) – Nov. 6), and the 11th month of China (7 Dec. – 4 Jan. 23) do not enable anybody to borrow money or acquire guarantees.

For the months that your finances have good liquidity, such as 2nd month of China (5 Mar. – 4 Apr.), 4th month of China (5 May. – 5 Jun), 6th month of China (7 Jul. – 6 Aug.), and the 7th month of China (7 Aug. – 6 Sep.).

Family

This year's family horoscope lacks harmony. There may be disagreements, confrontations, even geriatric health issues. Getting sick at home is a common occurrence. Also, keep an eye out for valuables that might be stolen or misplaced. Especially during the 3rd month of China (5 Apr. – 4 May), 8th month of China (7 Sep. – 7 Oct.), 9th month of China (8 Oct. – 6 Nov.), and the 11th month of China (7 Dec. – 4 Jan. 23) You must be cautious of unforeseen incidents that may result in injuries or bloodshed among the residents of the residence. Keep an eye out for misbehaving staff. You could also consider implementing a security system to keep others from taking your belongings. This year has been a letdown for family and friends. Both the good and the terrible will be present. Also, be wary about saying something that can offend people inadvertently. Especially during the 3rd month of China (5 Apr. – 4 May), the 8th month of China (7 Sep. – 7 Oct.), the 9th month of China (8 Oct. – 6

Nov.), and the 11th month of China (7 Dec. − 4 Jan. 23). You should avoid interfering in your friends' arguments during these months since they may be in danger. You must either avoid being exploited by your friends or being defamed by some of your pals.

Lover

The love horoscope for this year is favorable. Your partner will pay close attention to you. More people are willing to help, share, and empathize. Because you will have the opportunity to travel with your partner or spouse in luxury, allowing you to communicate and alter your understanding of what is stuck between you. But entering the 3rd month of China (5 Apr. − 4 May), 8th month of China (7 Sept. − 7 Oct.), 9th month of China (8 Oct. − 6 Nov.), and the 11th month of China (7 Dec. − 4 Jan. 23) are approaching. The fate must avoid visiting numerous entertainment establishments' celebrations. Because it will result in squabbles and mayhem. You should also avoid interfering in other people's households, which will lead to endless quarrels.

Health

Overall, this year's health is good. However, the fate must be cautious of work-related accidents or injuries caused by tools and road traffic. Accidents should be avoided, especially during the 3rd month of China (5 Apr. – 4 May), 8th month of China (7 Sep. – 7 Oct.), 9th month of China (8 Oct. – 6 Nov.), and the 11th month of China (7 Dec. – 4 Jan. 23). Machine tool operations must be done with caution and vigilance. If you're taking a prescription that makes you drowsy, you should pull over to the side of the road and find a safe spot to relax.

Lucky Numbers

7	4	3
5	0	8
6	4	1

Annual sacred objects for the Snake: "Guan Yu God bestows wealth "

Residential areas: should set sacred objects in the west.

Shop or workplace: Auspicious objects should be placed in the northwest.

* Should set the sacred object in the direction specified or facing the deity towards the door

Year of the Snake (Gold Element) (2001)

"Snake in the hibernation" Those born in the Year of the Snake Year of the Year, 19 years old (2001)

Overall Horoscope

For the teenage destiny of this age Because the planets orbiting into the streets, your life this year is the lawsuit, the affectionate star, and the young star. This will all result in causing headaches for you Therefore, knowing how to save yourself does not live on negligence so you do not fall into the trap. Is undermining one's future by using reason, Therefore, if you think of doing anything this year, do not be impatient. Consult an adult who has more experience than a safe solution. Better to be impatient than to know that is wrong. Damage and loss have already occurred. Because of the influence of the star litigation Often causing controversy and danger to the police station is a simple case. Beware of grouping with friends Maybe led to do bad things and cause trouble for others. The affection of the star affection Causing his destiny to be led to temptations and temptations Like to find pleasure Therefore may have a story follows, if you can avoid the place of orbiting, it's good. As well as having to know the rejection of friends that tend to lead to decadence Be careful of the arguments and crossfire from things that you do not cause. But must take responsibility Also, you must be careful of accidents and driving hazards. Use the car on the road.

Career

For teenagers Although this year, many bad stars are waiting to harass some obstacles hinder education. But if you are diligent and patient Determined not to give up Will be able to overcome obstacles and pass through During the months that the direction of work and learning is progressing is 12 Chinese months (6 Jan - 3 Feb), 4 Chinese months (5

May - 4 June), 8 Chinese months (7 Sep - 7 Oct) and 9 months in China (8 Oct - 6 Nov), although there are many good times for investing or investing in joint ventures. However, if consulting with some adults will help reduce the risk and reduce the chance of loss. During the months that the obstacles will encounter problems are 1 Chinese (4 Feb - 4 Mar), 5 Chinese (5 June - 5 July), 7 Chinese (7 Aug. .- 6 Sep), and 10 months in China (7 Nov - 5 Dec) that you will be affected by the bad group. Which will result in a lack of concentration in work The occurrence of problems and obstacles Work is often a conflict. Including meeting colleagues and retinue causing damage and trouble If some work has to be withdrawn, then it should be withdrawn. If stubborn, stubbornly careful to be damaged Signing various contract documents Should be considered carefully Be careful of the hidden minutiae. Also, the investment period should be delayed because there is a chance of being deceived. Including account fraud and bullying from some people.

Wealth

This year's financial fortune is a criterion for making a lot of money. Therefore, with the power of young people that carry a lot of energy, If you increase the diligence to eat Will receive a little reply During your financial months, the flow is good and smooth, namely Chinese 12 months (6 Jan - 3 Feb) 4 Chinese months (5 May - 4 June) 8 Chinese months (7 Kor November - 7 October) and 9 months in China (8 Oct - 6 Nov). However, you should not underestimate your spending. And should not gamble, gamble, or be greedy in the windfall, the results that others give Be careful to miss and lose your assets instead During the financial months, you will encounter a lack of liquidity such as 1 month in China (4 Feb - 4 March), 5 months in China (5 June - 5 July), 7 months in China (7 August - 6 September) and 10 months. China (7 Nov - 5 Dec) prohibits gambling. Do not give loans or sign financial guarantees. Do not invest in illegal businesses. And should not be greedy in the fortune received wrongfully Importantly, you should share some money to save in the event of an emergency.

Family

Within the family, even though this year there is auspicious power to sponsor visits But because this base was infested by the constellation Will result in health problems in the home. Home safety problems Problems in the house are quarreling with one another. Or going to have a story like a neighbor These problems will occur during the following months: 1st month of China (4 Feb - 4 Mar), 5th month of China (5 Jun - 5 July), 7th month of China (7 Aug - 6 Sep), and 10th month of China (7 Nov - 5 Dec) Beware of the small people lost valuable assets, lost or stolen by robbers.

Lover

For young people This year, you are quite charming. Will receive a lot of attention from the opposite sex But at a young age, There was still time for much thought and reflection. Better than urgently making a decision and causing mistakes and disappointments later. Although love is a matter of love If ever creating merit together would be a soul mate. If not then would have to be separated, therefore do not need to think too much In the months that love is quite fragile and can occur easily, such as the

1st Chinese month (4 Feb - 4 Mar), the 5th Chinese month (5 June - 5 July) month. 7 China (7 August - 6 September) and 10 months, China (7 Nov - 5 Dec). During this period, you must be mindful and direct and try not to behave uncontrollably. Or devoting time to a matter of neglecting to pay close attention to people Because will make arguments with the lover And may aggressively become a fractured relationship.

Health

Your health this year, at the beginning of the year and the end of the year, must add attention. Especially you must be extra careful on the head and face, as well as being careful to cause gastritis, intestinal diseases, pay attention to drinking hygiene May be found infected or exposed to toxic substances. Therefore should be kept clean and hygienic Especially during the months that you need to pay special attention to health care, such as the 1st month of China (4 Feb - 4 Mar), 5th month of China (5 June - 5 July), 7th month of China (7 Aug-6 Sep) and 10 months of China (7 Nov-5 Dec). Be extra careful of infectious diseases and other underlying diseases. Including being careful of injuries, bleeding, tires from accidents, both during work Or from using cars to use roads when traveling.

Lucky Numbers

7	2	5
8	9	3
0	1	4

Annual sacred objects for the Snake: " Guan Yu God bestows wealth "

Residence: Auspicious objects should be set to the West.

Shop or workplace: Auspicious objects should be placed in the Northwest.

* Should set the sacred object in the direction specified or facing the deity towards the door

Chinese Astrology Horoscope Each Month

Month 12 in the Ox Year
(6 January 2022 - 3 February 2022)

This month, the year of the snake moves into the alliance, and the route of life of fate, the year of the snake, moves into the alliance. Also, fortunate stars showed. Come in for a closer look to see how you can help. Like the sky when it rains and a gorgeous rainbow appears. Events It started to drift away. Work will go more smoothly. The trading firm will do well and make money. It's another time when auspicious power comes to visit, and it's a once-in-a-year opportunity.

What you should do at this period is work or make any investments you've ever dreamed of, and utilize your time this month as efficiently as possible. If funding, staff, and plans are available, take action to mold it. Do not waste time and do not allow this opportunity to pass you by.

This wage fortune is ripe for the picking. Incoming cash flow will be distributed in two ways. Money acquired by gambling, speculation, or luck is all earned through the use of one's hands. It should not, however, be greedy. It will not be worthwhile. What matters most is that you are diligent and determined.

Work is a source of wealth. Sponsorships from coworkers and adults are also available. As a result, you should not wait. Turn on the green light and proceed as planned to your destination. Because you will ponder, pause, and wait to choose if you think, hesitate, and wait.

Horoscope for a happy family Both may have added members or be having a good time to move into the house or a new dwelling place due to auspicious power to patronize the visit Able to manage auspicious work Both may have added members or be having a good time to move into the house or a new dwelling place due to auspicious power to patronize the visit

The season of love is when the love tree blooms. Enter the cottages or have a nice fortunate moment for the engagement.

For the sake of the family's riches, well health That dealing with severe situations may not be as difficult as anticipated since he will discover an expert who will propose a way out.

When starting new employment, enter stock information and make various investments, if possible.

Support Days: 5 Jan, 9 Jan, 13 Jan, 17 Jan, 21 Jan, 25 Jan, 29 Jan

Lucky Days: 12 Jan, 24 Jan

Moody Days: 3 Jan, 15 Jan, 27 Jan

Bad Days: 6 Jan, 18 Jan, 30 Jan

**Month 1 in the Tiger Year
(4 February 2022 - 4 March 2022)**
Your fortune has taken a turn for the worse since the Chinese New Year. As a result, there will be friction within the family. There will almost always be disagreements or

confrontations. You should also be aware of any illnesses among the household's members, as well as misplaced goods and mischievous children. As a result, it should devise a strategy to prevent and mitigate the catastrophe as soon as possible.

The income is minimal for this pay, but the costs are significant. Because the economy is still slow, you should establish a financial plan to distribute your budget for various activities. What you can save It's best to save it first. Should not invest in high-risk businesses or gamble, and should always keep an eye on the account.

Work involving paperwork, contracts, or other legal responsibilities. You must study it attentively and patiently to avoid any problems in the future.

Getting a new job or making an investment This isn't a nice situation right now. You'd best be patient.

Because love is in the middle of the month, if you are truly in love, you should approach and care for the other person consistently. Lovers will become frail with time.

Despite being in superb health, However, while traveling and working, be cautious of mishaps. may sustain an injury A menacing companion star intervenes in the fates of families and acquaintances. As a result, this month will be best spent apart. You're not going to get into any difficulty.

Support Days: 1 Feb, 5 Feb, 9 Feb, 13 Feb, 17 Feb, 21 Feb, 25 Feb

Lucky Days: 12 Feb, 24 Feb

Moody Days: 15 Feb, 27 Feb

Bad Days: 6 Feb, 18 Feb

Month 2 in the Tiger Year
(5 March 2022 - 4 April 2022)

This month, fortunate stars shine strongly in your destiny criterion. As a consequence, numerous issues and hurdles have been alleviated. Jobs in the trades will be aided. Assist in moving in the right path. Here's a list of things you should accomplish this month. Getting ready to build a portfolio and increase sales should be pursued to the utmost extent possible; there will be support channels available. Do as much as you can in a logical order. Above all, the job you perform must be of excellent quality. Don't only search for profit. To increase the market, both require talents, relationships, and intimate friendships.

This salary horoscope portends good fortune. You will have both direct and indirect income, as well as luck in another way. Because you may earn money in a multitude of ways. Make a nice living, but once you have it, you should be able to set aside a portion of it for spending. In this tranquil and pleasant month, the other half is to save, invest, and make charity for family activities.

This month, your body's health is fine, so don't be concerned.

This month in love, the path is strewn with rose petals, because those with open hearts will discover the ideal person they've been looking for.

Relatives and friends will enlist the aid of others, relying on both employment and financial support.

It is beneficial to collaborate or invest during this time. There will be prizes to be won.

Support Days: 1 Mar, 5 Mar, 9 Mar, 13 Mar, 17 Mar, 21 Mar, 25 Mar, 29 Mar

Lucky Days: 8 Mar, 20 Mar

Moody Days: 11 Mar, 23 Mar

Bad Days: 2 Mar, 14 Mar,26 Mar

Month 3 in the Tiger Year
(5 April 2022 - 4 May 2022)

This month, an unlucky star has been circling to annoy you. What was going well for you has stubbed its toe in the middle of the road and caused you harm. You should be wary of your emotions this month. Do not get irritated with others if the task has begun to generate issues; it will bring trouble. As a result, you must be able to manage your emotions. Don't be impatient or make a hasty decision. Because you would easily quarrel due to the haste. If you have any responsibilities, you should be able to fulfill them. It is preferable not to meddle with other people's jobs.

This salary's horoscopes fall on the seat and cost money. As a result, you must be cautious that liquidity does not suffer. Borrowing is illegal, as is obtaining guarantees. Don't take chances with your luck.

Obstacles were faced at work. The answer necessitates a positive relationship with others in your immediate vicinity. It may be important to seek assistance from others at times.

This month has been a difficult one for the family. Accidents and misplaced valuables should be avoided.

Injuries, bleeding, and rubber out should all be avoided. There will be difficulties and frustrations in love's destiny. So, for the sake of honesty, patience, and sacrifice, attempt to speak reasonably. It will be a powerful force in propelling a successful marriage, and most importantly, do not walk around the house because this will only exacerbate the love life problem. Joining and investing this month is not a good idea.

Support Days: 2 Apr, 6 Apr, 10 Apr, 14 Apr, 18 Apr, 22 Apr, 26 Apr, 30 Apr

Lucky Days: 1 Apr, 13 Apr, 25 Apr

Moody Days: 4 Apr, 16 Apr, 28 Apr

Bad Days: 7 Apr, 19 Apr

Month 4 in the Tiger Year
(5 May 2022 - 5 June 2022)

The horoscope trend for this month has also obtained favorable strength, causing it to surge consistently. Business and trade are continuing to run well. Here's a list of things you should accomplish this month. In addition to being a trailblazer in terms of expanding and increasing sales. To avoid missing out on possibilities, you should implement a management system inside your business to support the task at the same time. Changes in preparation for the base adjustment that will grow in the future can be seen in the work area. Both bosses and subordinates should have work that is tailored to them. To establish a positive working connection that will aid in the smooth flow of work while also fostering a sense of oneness, which will bring about the strength of management.

For this salary horoscope, little income means more spending. As a result, it's vital to save money on seat belts. Avoid gambling and try to cut down on needless spending.

This month's family horoscope is still typical, pleasant, and healthy. However, while traveling, you must be cautious of mishaps.

This month's love side is delightful. Relationships become entwined in a web of affection until all that is heard are pleasant words.

Relatives and friends appear to be in good health. You have the option of going on adventures or working together.

When it comes to investing, there is a shining path that may be taken.

Support Days: 4 May, 8 May, 12 May, 16

May, 20 May, 24 May, 28 May

Lucky Days: 7 May, 19 May, 31 May

Moody Days: 10 May, 22 May

Bad Days: 1 May, 13 May, 25 May

Month 5 in the Tiger Year
(6 June 2022 - 6 July 2022)

This month's criterion for your fate is still shifting. It's also impossible to predict where the administration will go in the future.

Here's a list of things you should accomplish this month. Trying to build a culture of justice and fairness in the company for the general public to have peace by taking care of your obligations as well as you can to reduce disputes and settle differences.

Salary horoscopes continue to plummet and show no signs of improvement. As a result, you'll need to be extremely frugal with your money. They must be wary of being duped by unscrupulous individuals. Consider where you should put your money. must be thoroughly investigated Don't fall for the small prey that others provide in the trap because you're greedy. will result in a significant financial loss

Contracting that might be abused should be avoided during this time. should take time to read and research.

There are still some troubling and unsatisfying aspects in this month's household. People in the residence will be wounded if the machine tool is used. Also, be wary of thief hazards.

The state of my health is not excellent. While traveling, keep an eye out for gastritis, intestinal sickness, and accidents.

This month is not excellent in terms of love. Arguments are easy to start when someone is mentally unstable and easily agitated.

This month's destiny for family and friends is mild. If you invest in something that isn't beneficial for you, you have the right to be misleading and lose money.

Support Days: 1 Jun, 5 Jun, 9 Jun, 13 Jun, 17 Jun, 21 Jun, 25 Jun, 29 Jun

Lucky Days: 12 Jun, 24 Jun

Moody Days: 3 Jun, 15 Jun, 27 Jun

Bad Days: 6 Jun, 18 Jun, 30 Jun

**Month 6 in the Tiger Year
(7 July 2022 - 6 August 2022)**
This month, though, your life will take a turn

for the better. Internal roadblocks, though, remain. This month, you should seek guidance from experts on how to fix the situation. You must also be trustworthy and dedicated to your task. Stick to your goals and learn how to use technology to help you react to changing circumstances. As a result, it will aid in the removal of numerous job-related difficulties. Even though this era is full of hurdles and demands, you will be able to overcome them in the end if you have the drive to do so. Do it gradually and consistently. The troubled wall will be shattered, and you will triumph and stand high once more.

Because your compensation is balanced, you will have some money left over, but not much. However, you should share a percentage of your earnings to save, and you should not enable people to borrow money or accept guarantees.

The fortunes of this family are better.

Physical health, despite certain sicknesses, but they need to locate a competent doctor and excellent treatment to recover swiftly from illness. However, the importance of eating and living should not be overlooked. During the voyage, be cautious of food sickness and accidents.

In terms of love, despite certain arguments, they continue to support each other well.

Before going, investments must also be carefully assessed.

Support Days: 3 Jul, 7 Jul, 11 Jul, 15 Jul, 19 Jul, 23 Jul, 27 Jul, 31 Jul

Lucky Days: 6 Jul, 18 Jul, 30 Jul

Moody Days: 9 Jul, 21 Jul

Bad Days: 12 Jul, 24 Jul

Month 7 in the Tiger Year
(7 August 2022 - 6 September 2022)

This month, your fate has shifted to a more favorable month. There are also a lot of lucky stars that have congregated to shine brilliantly. As a consequence, whatever is tough will be aided by a sponsor. This month, focus on clearing your backlog and resolving any past issues. Make one more sale and prepare for the construction of a portfolio.

The wealthy will be eligible to acquire additional money from gambling in exchange for this pay. because, in a prosperous era Rather than going on vacations and blowing your money, you can put it to good use. The principles for benefiting from assets should be applied to accomplish the following five goals:

1. to look after oneself, one's family, and one's parents.

2. It is used to feed friends and coworkers.

3. Keep it on hand for when you need it since you never know when an accident will happen.

4. Giving up possessions to assist family members

5. It was used to make merit, revere religion, and devote it to one's parents.

If you can do this, you may consider yourself to be making excellent use of your assets, and it is a beneficial use both now and in the future.

This month is straightforward and satisfying

within your household.

Don't be concerned about your health; you are not sick.

You enjoy favorable occasions for betrothal, marriage, childbirth, and auspicious job throughout this season of love.

Investing or collaborating during this time will have a positive future.

Support Days: 4 Aug, 8 Aug, 12 Aug, 16 Aug, 20 Aug, 24 Aug, 28 Aug

Lucky Days: 11 Aug, 23 Aug

Moody Days: 2 Aug, 14 Aug, 28 Aug

Bad Days: 5 Aug, 17 Aug, 29 Aug

**Month 8 in the Tiger Year
(7 September 2022 - 7 October 2022)**
This month, your luck has changed

drastically. You will confront several challenges. Work and trading are difficult. in addition to being assaulted by foes Here's a list of things you should accomplish this month. You must learn to adapt to the demanding situation. Let's look at the income and spending account first. Any account that has a residue or an issue should contact us right away. Simultaneously, you must endeavor to increase your revenue while slowing payments to ensure that there is still liquidity in the system.

This is not a favorable salary horoscope. Because there will be a monetary leak. As a result, you must be cautious about bribery and unanticipated losses. Furthermore, gambling and gambling should be avoided. Make sure you don't get into too much debt. Be wary of bad debts and management line disputes, since they may cause issues and cause you to become trapped at work.

This month has been very difficult for the family. Arguments arising from differences must be avoided. The ideal method is to speak slowly and avoid stretching the girl's length; the stretch will be more effective. Also, be wary of the elderly. Blood spurts out from an injured servant in a burglary house.

This month's love side is delightful. Empathy and concern for one's health are admirable qualities, yet one must use caution when it comes to one's health. It can induce gastritis, intestinal sickness, headaches, fainting, and bodily discomfort, and travelers should be aware of the risks.

Support Days: 1 Sep, 5 Sep, 9 Sep, 13 Sep, 17 Sep, 21 Sep, 25 Sep, 29 Sep

Lucky Days: 4 Sep, 16 Sep, 28 Sep

Moody Days: 7 Sep, 19 Sep

Bad Days: 10 Sep, 22 Sep

Month 9 in the Tiger Year
(8 October 2022 - 6 November 2022)

This month, destiny's path bounces up and down, making it insecure. Job responsibilities and crafts are frequently investigated and questioned. What you must remember on this occasion is not to be overly greedy. It should only be carried out once. Especially if it is governed by a contract, is over-capacity, or is carried out on something that cannot be regulated independently. You should decline. Otherwise, it may cause harm. And since the work will change this month. If the system and management are not up to par, the organization has the right to lose. As a result, you should utilize your expertise and care to inquire about individuals with experience to ensure the long-term viability of your company.

This is sufficient in terms of remuneration. The money keeps coming in. However, there is still a significant chance of fortune drifting. As a result, don't take any chances with your money.

Food poisoning must be avoided at all costs in health care. Blood pressure and diabetes-related diseases will be asked about.

Love is not a nice thing. Misunderstandings are frequently the source of disagreements. As a result, you should avoid visiting amusement parks and instead spend more time with your loved ones to assist alleviate the situation.

During this time, be wary of family and friends who may be duped or cause difficulty, so they may need to keep their distance. You should also avoid making any investments this month.

Support Days: 3 Oct, 7 Oct, 11 Oct, 15 Oct, 19 Oct, 23 Oct, 27 Oct, 31 Oct

Lucky Days: 10 Oct, 22 Oct

Moody Days: 1 Oct, 13 Oct, 25 Oct

Bad Days: 4 Oct, 16 Oct, 28 Oct

Month 10 in the Tiger Year
(7 November 2022 - 6 December 2022)

This month, your horoscope is likely to improve. Obstacles you've faced in the past will fade away with time. You may build a portfolio and diversify your trading. The most important thing for you to accomplish is to remain persistent in your quest for information. Take advantage of technology to assist you. Let's talk about it a little more because there's a destiny promotion going on. In this magnificent month, it's all about hard work and destiny. It will enable you to locate good job chances in your sector. You should also unify the organization and build positive relationships with trade partners. To get out of the difficulty, plan to increase revenues and drain several items that are remaining in the warehouse.

With improved liquidity, this salary will flow effortlessly. The family will be informed of the excellent news. However, be wary of ill-wishers who may show up and cause havoc.

To avoid disagreements in love, strive to keep your emotions under control.

To maintain good health, you should be aware of illnesses and injuries caused by accidents.

The fates of family and acquaintances were likewise tainted by the presence of harmful companion stars. Even if you are not busy, you must be aware that there will be quarrels and quarrels. However, they may be struck by crossfire, wreaking.

Support Days: 4 Nov, 8 Nov, 12 Nov, 16 Nov, 20 Nov, 24 Nov, 28 Nov

Lucky Days: 3 Nov, 15 Nov, 27 Nov

Moody Days: 6 Nov, 18 Nov, 30 Nov

Bad Days: 9 Nov, 21 Nov

Month 11 in the Tiger Year (7 December 2022 - 4 January 2023)

Due to your destiny criterion being plagued by bad stars this month, as well as destiny entering a detrimental zodiac month, putting great strain on your job tasks, all of your responsibilities have been unstable, as if the monsoons were coming in faster and faster. Make all of your job and commerce operations confront difficulties and challenges that you must constantly follow and address. Bad debt was discovered by the accounting system, or there was an account decoration. As a result, you must maintain your composure to deal with the mayhem that will ensue.

On the salary front, this falls on the seat and the property is lost. As a result, you should not continue to gamble. Furthermore, do not engage in criminal activity or infringe on the rights of others. Because there are requirements that will be penalized and may be charged criminally.

This step should carefully evaluate the nuances of various contracts. because it may be deceived. Being taken advantage of or having a burdensome commitment. Also, be wary about being attacked and bullied.

Support Days: 2 Dec, 6 Dec, 10 Dec, 14 Dec, 18 Dec, 22 Dec, 26 Dec, 30 Dec

Lucky Days: 9 Dec, 21 Dec

Moody Days: 12 Dec, 24 Dec

Bad Days: 3 Dec, 15 Dec, 27 Dec

Amulet for Snake Year

" Guan Yu God bestows wealth "

Those who were born in the Snake year this year should create and worship sacred artifacts. To improve fortune, "God Guan Yu bestows money." By placing it on a desk or a cash register, you are requesting His Majesty's assistance in protecting destiny from all the troubles that will arise as a consequence of the unlucky stars that will collide this year and ruin it. born under good circumstances, full of riches and wealth all year

(Note: religious things should be established in a certain orientation.) After your life cycle, you may see it in the text.)

Chapter one of the Department of Advanced Feng Shui discusses the deities that will descend to dwell in the yearly Mi Keng (Destiny House), who are gods who may bring both good and harm to the year's destiny. When this is the case, worshiping to increase your luck with gods who visit in the same year as your birth is said to be the most helpful and impacting you. to be able to rely on the gods' esteem Assist in the protection of your destiny when it is deteriorating and misery is being relieved. At the same time, Thun requests your blessing to assist you in conducting business as smoothly as possible. Bring you and your family happiness and wealth.

Ji is the zodiac sign of those born in the year of the Snake or Mi Keng (House of Destiny). This is going to be a challenging year for you. You will be disappointed if you rely on others. To be good, you must do everything yourself. It's OK if you're a company owner or have a full-time job. If you don't want to be tricked this year, do what you're capable of and don't blindly trust anyone. Aside from the year of his birth, another year has had a role in the Tai Tai tribute's significance. Even though a patron star is on hand to assist, However, there are still more issues and roadblocks than smoothness, trading ups and downs, and insecure positions. And there will almost always be a financial loss as a result of unwise expenditures. You must also use caution in your words and interpersonal interactions. Bullying and violence should be avoided. You will easily discover a nice lifemate this year. However, the wedding had to be postponed. Because this is not the year to make a long-term commitment to anyone. Take care of your health if you're suffering from headaches, stomachaches, or heart issues. Some of you will have to have surgery. They must be cautious that the adults in the house do not become unwell. You should establish and worship if you want to solve calamities. "God Guan Yu bestows wealth" is a request for the strength of his prestige to aid destiny in escaping all perils. Make an excellent career growth and a successful trade. Money flows and thinks about anything, yearning for it to be accomplished in the way that it is wanted.

Character, according to God Guan Yu, is a person who maintains his promise with his life, values virtue and honesty and is loyal to his benefactor. He wields an 82-pound halberd, rides a skillful warhorse named "Chek Tao," and has two trustworthy

warlords named "Guan Peng" and "Jiwong."
He is revered as the god of honesty and
justice by both Chinese and Thai people.
Defend against all manner of wicked and
perilous situations. as well as provide good
fortune Households and families benefit from
wealth. You're a god of triumph, too. (Battle a
hundred times, win a hundred times), so
increasing the rule's prestige, leading the
bullies to flee and prospering prosperity.

Additionally, persons born in the Snake year
should wear a lucky pendant. When traveling
both near and far, wear "The God Guan Yu
bestows wealth" around your neck or take it
with you. as a result of which your future is
filled with entire fortunate prosperity. Both
business and trade are flourishing and
progressing. Year-round happiness in the
family leads to increased efficiency and
production.

The auspicious direction: southeast,
west, and southwest
The unfortunate direction: northwest

The Lucky colors of the Rat: red, pink,

orange, bright, and green.

Good Luck Time: 09.00 - 10.59. 15.00 - 16.59. 17.00 - 18.59.
Bad Time to avoid: 03.00 - 04.59, 21.00 - 22.59

Good Luck
2022

www.ingramcontent.com/pod-product-compliance
Lightning Source LLC
Chambersburg PA
CBHW060443160726
47992CB00003B/1049